carte blanche
greetings ltd ®

www.carteblanchegreetings.com

First edition for the United States published in 2010 by Barron's Educational Series, Inc.

First published in the U.K. by HarperCollins Children's Books in 2008 under the title:
Me to You—To the One I Love.

All inquiries should be addressed to:
Barron's Educational Series, Inc.
250 Wireless Boulevard
Hauppauge, NY 11788
www.barronseduc.com

ISBN-13: 978-0-7641-6342-5
ISBN-10: 0-7641-6342-6

Printed in China

9 8 7 6 5 4 3 2 1

To the One I Love

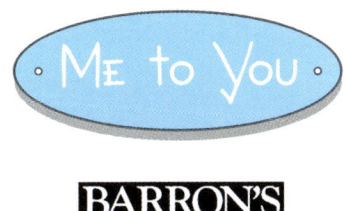

BARRON'S

WITH love
today and always.

When I'm with you,
nothing else matters.

I want you to know
just how much
I love you!

You always know
how to make me feel
so special.

I'm lost without you.

Words can't describe
my love for you.

All the special things
you do mean so much.

You are simply...
my everything!

Your love is
the greatest gift of all.

Being with you
warms my heart.

You fill my dreams
with love.

You have my heart today, tomorrow, and forever!